*The Girl I Once Was
and Other Poems*

The Girl I Once Was and Other Poems

Kristi Bishop

RESOURCE *Publications* · Eugene, Oregon

THE GIRL I ONCE WAS AND OTHER POEMS

Copyright © 2025 Kristi Bishop. All rights reserved. Except for brief quotations in critical publications or reviews, no part of this book may be reproduced in any manner without prior written permission from the publisher. Write: Permissions, Wipf and Stock Publishers, 199 W. 8th Ave., Suite 3, Eugene, OR 97401.

Resource Publications
An Imprint of Wipf and Stock Publishers
199 W. 8th Ave., Suite 3
Eugene, OR 97401

www.wipfandstock.com

PAPERBACK ISBN: 979-8-3852-6135-2
HARDCOVER ISBN: 979-8-3852-6136-9
EBOOK ISBN: 979-8-3852-6137-6

VERSION NUMBER 10/09/25

For Roddy

Contents

Preface | ix
Acknowledgments | xi
Introduction | xiii

My Story Is Jesus | 1
The Morning Sun | 3
Life's Hourglass | 5
Wild, Wondrous Wind | 7
What Was There All the Time | 9
Goodnight | 11
The Hawk | 13
Overtaken by Springtime | 15
Rainbow of Hope | 17
Alabama Snowfall | 19
Heaven Enough for Me | 21
Take Time to Take It All In | 23
Moonlight on the Water | 25
Evergreen Love | 27
When the Clouds Start Glowing at Sundown | 30
Four-Leaf Clover Prayer | 32
Look Around | 35
It Calls to Me | 38
Don't Forget to Look for the Moon | 40
Our Heavenly Father Feeds Them | 42

I'll Be Here | 44

River of Clouds | 47

Woodland Cathedral | 49

The Bottle of Tears | 51

The Peach and Purple Sunset | 53

Thank You, Lord, for the Light | 55

So, He Gave Me You | 57

I Can't Let You Go | 59

Rainy July Day | 61

Have You Ever Had a Friend | 63

Blow, Wind, Blow | 65

Nature's Voice | 67

Goodbye, Old Oak | 69

The Girl I Once Was | 71

Kings of the Air | 74

Beauty in the Darkness | 76

Peggy's Poem | 78

How Beautiful Heaven Must Be | 81

New Year's Eve | 83

The Brave and Hopeful Beauty of the Soul | 85

Preface

I NEVER KNOW WHEN an idea for poetry will suddenly strike me, and I am quick to record short phrases or an entire poem before I forget. I have dozens of titles and first lines jotted down on yellow sticky notes stuffed into a tattered envelope. Thankfully, there is no end in sight to these unanticipated thoughts, and writing poetry remains one of my most enjoyable, rewarding activities.

From scribbles and words that I text to myself, my poems progress to being written down in entirety on notebook paper. I may change the order of the verses for a more logical sequence, but the rhyming lines are only typed on my laptop once I am satisfied with every word. In the clarity of printed form, I occasionally find an adjective or phrase that needs modification, and then each creation is complete. When commenting to my husband about my unsophisticated composition methods, his valid response was, "Whatever works."

Although both the verses and the introduction for each poem are written in blue ink on college-ruled lines, an extreme contrast exists between the two elements. Writing poetry comes easily, naturally, and spontaneously to me. Writing the paragraphs preceding the poems is challenging, requiring concerted effort and discipline. Editing these passages is even more tedious, requiring many hours of word wrestling before I send them to my sister, Tina, for her professional, effortless alterations. But in the end, all this work affords me an amazing opportunity to share and connect with my readers. I am humbled by this priceless reward.

Acknowledgments

I WOULD LIKE TO thank my sister, Tina Frist Smith, for editing the prose in this volume. Her gracious generosity as much as her exceptional skill are deeply appreciated. This superior version of the book would not exist without her contribution. My writing ability is specific to poetry. I simply do not have her talent of expertly molding the English language into exquisite sentences and paragraphs, like a potter with clay. She also assisted me with writing applications to publishers, biographical pieces used for marketing, and the information found on the back of this collection.

For many reasons, I would like to acknowledge my mom, Dolly Collier. She remains my biggest fan and is genuinely delighted with each new poem I share. Mom is also a faithful marketer of my books. She has purchased dozens of volumes and given the books to friends and acquaintances. But even more appreciated is Mom's relating to me the positive responses she receives from the recipients. This feedback thrills my heart and provides the motivation and confidence I need to continue growing as a writer. It is absolutely a dream come true to know people are reading and enjoying my poetry.

This book is dedicated to my precious husband of nearly four decades, Roddy. His patience and enduring support during my mental health relapses have been crucial, and I owe so much to him. I am also extremely grateful for his charming ways, affectionate nature, cheerful personality, wonderful sense of humor, and steadfast devotion. I love him with all my heart.

Finally, I am forever indebted to God, my Creator, Father, and Friend, who catches my tears in a bottle, never leaves my side, and persistently infuses my life with beauty and joy.

Introduction

NATURE IS MY MUSE. She is like a living being to me, thrilling my heart every day and inspiring dozens of poems. In my last two books she heavily supported my creativity. Nature continues her role in this volume, but in many of the poems she is not the star. Instead, my words flow from deep, poignant, and even painful emotions. I pray these verses do not sadden you.

Most people I interact with at work, church, and other social settings are unaware of the battle I have fought with depression since my mid-20's. Mental illness has a strong presence on both sides of my family, and unfortunately, I have also been affected by this challenging condition. I am an expert at putting on a happy mask during periods of relapse and extremely skilled at hiding the feelings of pain and even despair that I experience during these dark seasons. Very few people know that there have been several occasions over the past three decades when I have been a danger to myself. Many times, I have groped my way through the long, dark tunnel that runs under a mountain of despondency and anxiety, clinging to the hand of Jesus. Through his grace and with medical attention I have triumphantly emerged, squinting in the brilliant light of mental wellness. In wonder and gratitude, I have again embraced hope.

As I face the future it is easy to fear the return of these agonizing episodes, but I truly believe that I am cupped in God's hand continually, and that he shields me from the evil one. This brings me the peace that is so vital to a happy, creative, and productive life, one in which I can connect with those around me and hopefully make this world a better place. I crave this connection and influence not only with the people I interact with physically but also with the ones my poetry reaches. I recognize the relative insignificance of my books, but I pray that the few individuals who read them will experience not only joy, but comfort and hope. If something I have written helps even one person, I am satisfied. My poems are almost like children to me, each one holding a special place in my heart, so all my books are very precious to me. But because of its deeply personal nature, this collection of verses is my favorite. With realness and rawness, I share more of myself than I ever have before.

My Story Is Jesus

Although the present is precious, and the future should hold our focus, there can also be significant value in looking back over our lives. Not with regret or sadness, but to identify and celebrate the wonderful working of God, remembering times when he helped us through challenges, brought us tremendous joy, kept his many promises, and taught us important lessons. As I reflect on my past, I see all this and much more. I observe trials and anxiety I thought would never end that are now a distant memory. I recognize times when my Heavenly Father told me "No" or "Wait" and I'm grateful he did. I identify experiences which felt like failures but were signposts to help me find my way. I discern disappointments later revealed to be blessings. I perceive mistakes that were extremely educational. Most of all I see the Lord's grace, guidance, and favor. God is the author of my life story. I tremble to imagine the plot without the pen in his hand. And even though I may not know how the next chapter reads, I am confident of how the book ends.

"Everyone has a story," I've oft heard it said.
Those events that we might think define us.
Tragedy, triumph, failure, success,
Or something we can't leave behind us.

Stories as different as the prints we can make
With fingertips unique to each human.
But the journey so common to all of mankind
For some will restore, and some ruin.

My story with all of its various chapters,
Characters, conflicts, and plots,
Tends to profoundly and purely distill
Into one simple all reaching thought:

That my story is Jesus. His presence, his love,
Can be seen on each yellowing page.
Tho some may be tear-stained, he's there just the same.
He's the star of my life's center stage.

Jesus has guided and guarded my steps,
Whether seen or unseen by my heart.
Between all the lines you can read what he's said.
In each paragraph, he plays a part.

Yes, my story is Jesus, and as it unfolds,
The ending I've known all along.
It's a fairy-tale finish, we finally embrace,
And I'm home where I've always belonged.

The Morning Sun

I FREQUENTLY ADMIRE AND write about the radiant moon, but I also maintain tremendous appreciation for the marvelous center of our solar system. The sun's warmth allows humans and our magnificent natural world to thrive. It illuminates the many colors and textures around us, produces rainbows, and cheers cold winter days. That golden orb creates mesmerizing patterns as its rays filter through the leaves of trees, causes the edges of clouds it hides behind to glow silver and gold, and makes rivers and oceans sparkle. Travelling across the heavens, the sun marks the hours of days and the days of years while painting stunning sunrises and sunsets on the horizons. After the dark night, how welcome the sunlight is when it finally appears! Its arrival wakes us, invigorates us, and instills hope in our hearts. When you see the morning sun, greet the Creator of this distant star with gratitude, remembering that not everyone woke up to live another day basking in its light.

It's a morning like no other,
Except in Eden's bliss.
I see the glowing hilltops that
The rising sun has kissed.

The earth is warmed and lighted,
And the sleeping birds awake,
Lifting heads from under wings
And giving them a shake.

The trees and flowers smile and beam
And stand a little higher,
So far below the lifeforce of
That distant solar fire.

All nature basks in wonder
At the long night's welcome end
And the streaming rays the daytime king
So effortlessly sends.

As a hushed anticipation
Pervades the whole outdoors,
I'm inspired to question hopefully
What this bright day has in store.

Life's Hourglass

There is a wide, tranquil freedom to be found when we truly entrust our lives to God. When we faithfully accept his wise answers to our prayers and rest in his strong arms like a child nestled in the arms of a loving parent. When we calmly acknowledge the perfection of his timing, holding onto him firmly in hours of darkness. It may take a lifetime of observing, experiencing, and learning to believe that God is unquestionably trustworthy. This conviction will not only affect our thought processes but also how we spend our time. We will understand that our season on earth is brief compared to eternity and endeavor to use each moment to honor the Lord. We will see the preciousness of our days while not fearing the end of our days. Death is not the worst thing that can happen to us. Living without purpose, peace, and hope is a far greater calamity and perhaps the greatest tragedy of all.

Life's hourglass cannot be turned over
Once the sand that is ours starts to run.
Nothing can stop it or slow it.
There's no going back once it's done.

Each grain is a brief, sacred moment
That moves through the glass and the day
At a speed which we so often question.
"Where does the time go?" we might say.

Our number of grains was determined
Long before we all first took in air

By the one who both made and sustains us
And keeps us so close in his care.

He knows what is best for his children.
We can trust that his timing's not flawed.
For before the sand flows through the hourglass,
It sifts through the fingers of God.

Wild, Wondrous Wind

A HURRICANE IN THE Gulf of Mexico delivered several days of clouds, rain, and thunderstorms to North Alabama. The first day of this stretch of unpleasant weather lent itself to a curious, strong wind, accompanied by scattered sprinkles of rain. From sunup to sundown a constant gale brought down clusters of leaves, small branches, and hundreds of sticks and pinecones from the numerous trees in my neighborhood, leaving copious debris to litter the driveways and yards while scurrying across streets. My four-foot-tall, pink and orange zinnias leaned at an alarming angle, requiring additional bracing with stakes and ties to prevent their stems from breaking. Walking in this atmosphere was exhilarating and exciting. The blustery wind alternately pushed and pulled me along my route. I was amazed at nature's impressive power and wondered what it must be like to experience an actual hurricane.

It was a long, strange day, with the wild wind keeping my attention focused on the chaos outside. I paused often to gaze out the windows, marvel at the swaying trees, and note any rainfall. In the evening, I ventured outside again to check my trembling flowers, and my worried son soon followed and urged me to come back inside. I reluctantly complied. Long after I could see only gloomy blackness beyond my windows, the rowdy wind persisted, and at bedtime it sang me to sleep with its boisterous melody.

I enjoyed the strange, windy weather today,
Caused by a hurricane south,
But much like the three little pigs with the wolf
I thought it might blow down my house.

The wind never ceased, it never ran out,
And I listened all day to the sound
Of it moving the treetops, roaring away,
And knocking debris to the ground.

The rainless, gray clouds hung so heavy and low,
The sunlight could hardly break through.
It was somber and eerie, majestic and odd,
And somehow quite wonderful, too.

I went out for a walk with the gusts at my back,
And then blowing right in my face.
I watched the commotion they caused in the trees.
I watched the leaves tumble and race.

The wind seemed to carry me back to my yard
To secure all my tall, swaying flowers.
Once safe inside, I listened to all
Of my tinkling windchimes for hours.

As night fell the rowdy gale only increased.
Louder and louder, it groaned.
The wind had become a person to me,
Who it seemed that I always had known.

I crawled into bed but the wind didn't rest,
And I bid it a sleepy "Goodnight."
I wondered, "Will my friend still be here
When I wake with the new morning light?"

What Was There All the Time

I WAS FLYING ON a gloomy, overcast day to join my husband in Washington state for a vacation. Several years had passed since I'd flown on an airplane, and I was thrilled to have booked a window seat. Glued to that small, scratched portal from takeoff to cruising altitude, I observed an astonishing transformation. Moments after lifting off the runway, the aircraft broke through a thick layer of gray clouds into glorious sunshine. Not expecting such a vivid contrast, I was surprised at the close proximity of the dazzling light. Alone with my thoughts, the object lesson was crystal clear and highly familiar: during the dark seasons of life, shining hope exists just beyond the shadows. Clouds may obscure the sun, but they cannot extinguish it. Although we are unable to visualize better days, they will inevitably come. Hard times do not last forever. When you are sad and struggling, remember that sunshine is nearer than you might think.

Above the dark clouds, the sun's shining.
I know for a fact that it's true.
I just rode a plane on a rainy, gray day
Up and up to the yonder bright blue.

Up here there are clouds, but they're radiant puffs,
In a layer it seems I could stand on.
A soft, cozy bed made of pillows so dense
Or a surface that something could land on.

Higher and higher we continue to climb,
And the layers become mountains tattered.
White jagged peaks and snowy round domes,
And a billow that's shaped much like Saturn.

The azure up here is different and clear.
There're no words that begin to describe
The perfect, pure hue that I try to take in
With my soul just as much as my eyes.

So the next time it seems the tears never will end,
And heartache will always be mine,
I'll remember the day I flew up through the rain
And found what was there all the time.

Goodnight

I began composing "Goodnight" while walking outside on a stuffy summer evening. I had been unable to take my usual morning stroll, and by evening I was craving movement and the profound peace that nature provides. Returning home just before darkness fell, I observed the outdoors as the warm day ended. This unique setting was pervaded with feelings of gradual deceleration, collective calm, and reluctant closure. I rarely schedule poem writing; instead, unexpected ideas and phrases waltz into my mind as effortlessly as professional dancers glide across the dance floor. Most of my poetry is simply a response to what I experience or feel, as opposed to a task to be completed. With these verses the process was no different. I texted a few phrases to myself as I walked, and when I reached my house was able to write these words down freely and joyfully.

Daylight is reluctantly fading,
As nighttime creeping comes.
For rabbits, one last nibble.
For bees, a few more hums.

The birds are turning quiet.
I don't hear many songs.
Some little flowers petals close
Until the break of dawn.

When it says "goodnight," even the sun
As below horizon sinks,

Can rest now from its shining work—
Or at least I'd like to think.

The hour has come for all to rest,
Both great and small, and me,
To find a sheltered place to sleep
In water, ground, or tree

Or cozy bed, in house so snug,
Then peaceful dreams can take
Us through the sacred, velvet dark
Till joyful sunlight wakes.

The Hawk

A DEEP SENSE OF belonging and complete fulfillment will elude humanity as long as we are pinned to this planet by gravity. People were originally placed in a perfect, sinless garden to walk and talk with God in person. Currently aliens in a foreign land, physically separated from our Heavenly Father, earthlings cannot help but be underachievers. But this state of less-than will not last forever. Someday mortals will fulfill their true calling, living not only in a place more glorious than Eden but also once again in God's continual, tangible presence. The human race was created for infinitely more than we experience during our brief lives here on Earth. In spirit and in body, we were literally born to fly.

A lone hawk soars above me
With wingbeats very rare,
Held up by rising currents,
He can't see, without a care.

Beyond the reach of earthlings,
A dot against the blue,
Gliding under shreds of clouds
With sunlight shining through.

Alone he sails, much like a ship
Solitary on a sea.
You'd think he might be lonely,
But he's clearly content to be

So high, and oh, so tranquil.
It must be quiet there,
A thousand feet above
The noise and struggle we all share.

In mind I'm right there with him,
And how my spirit flies.
It rises, up and up
until my soul's one with the sky.

And like the hawk, I'm peaceful.
I could stay there evermore,
Ascending steadily higher
Till I knock on heaven's door.

Overtaken by Springtime

THIS POEM WAS INSPIRED by a text I received from my dad. Like me, he is a passionate lover of nature and a keen observer of the magnificent and intriguing world that awaits us every time we step outdoors. He lives out in the country on a picturesque piece of property, and he often texts me short descriptions of the beautiful environment that surrounds him. One year as Spring descended upon the earth in all her glory, he sent a message. Tediously typed out on his flip phone, it read, "I am overtaken by Springtime. Trees are in full bloom." I absolutely loved his admission that his heart had been so acutely touched by the magical finger of this vibrant season. That feeling of wonder is something not everyone understands, and it's a delight to find a kindred spirit. Prompted by this comradery my dad and I share, I picked up my pen to compose. The resulting verses echo Dad's words along with our shared appreciation of nature's countless gifts.

I am overtaken by Springtime.
The trees are a white blaze of blooms.
The birds have assembled a choir
And delight me with bright little tunes.

The green of the trees and the grasses
Is a shade I can hardly define.
It possesses the essence of newness
And a quality almost divine.

The season's rare beauty distracts me
From completing the tasks of the day.
I linger outside in the sunshine
And carefully soak up each ray.

The damp woodland path seems to call me.
I wonder how it knows my name.
The delicate flowers along it
Assure me they're glad that I came.

The daffodils nod a shy greeting,
Standing so fresh in their prime.
They won't be this lovely tomorrow;
Their blossoms will grow dim with time.

Yes, Springtime will all too soon vanish,
And nature's next season will start.
But today I can treasure her glory
And store up her joys in my heart.

Rainbow of Hope

TRIALS AND HARDSHIP WERE not a part of God's original plan for humans but unfortunately are experienced by every person on this rogue planet. We may be tempted to question why the Lord allows suffering to invade our lives. Even with an understanding of the great controversy between good and evil that wages daily, it takes faith to trust that God is just, wise, loving, and still in control. A complete understanding of God's workings is not possible until we are in heaven, when our eyes will be opened. Until then we can weather life's storms confidently, assured that our Heavenly Father will never leave us and will always see us through. Once all is revealed, we will look back on our lives with wonder, thanking our gracious Savior for bringing us safely home.

The storm in my life is subsiding.
I think that I might make it through.
Up there in the gray clouds above me
Do I see a sliver of blue?

The merciless gale is now dying,
As a warm, gentle breeze takes its place.
The hesitant sun is emerging
And shining on my tear-stained face.

Though weary and worn I'm still standing,
And my tired eyes open to see
The rainbow of hope that's now glowing,
As the grip of the storm sets me free.

My healing might be slow in coming,
Like a stem that must push through the earth.
Through soil that's been moistened with struggle
I come forth to claim my rebirth.

For now I will thank God for sunshine,
And days that are temperate and fair.
I'm stronger to face the next tempest.
In the midst of it all he'll be there.

Alabama Snowfall

I WAS BORN IN Ohio and experienced harsh winters and ample snow as a child. A blizzard in 1976 brought five-foot snowdrifts to Indiana, where I was living at the time. Now I prefer mild winter months, having resided in Alabama for more than thirty-five years. But one thing I dislike about wintertime in the Heart of Dixie is the brown lawns. The Bermuda and Zoysia grasses that are common here resemble light green velvet in the summer, but then dirty, tan carpet during cold months. This is why I insisted our yard be sodded with Fescue grass, even though it is more difficult and costly to maintain. My lawn stays miraculously green even when the temperatures drop, because I just can't bear to look out my windows at tawny drabness for weeks at a time.

The day before I wrote this poem our region was christened with four inches of exquisite, fluffy snow. It erased the dreary brownness of the landscape, covering everything with a sparkling white blanket. The boxwoods resembled marshmallows; the sloping roofs looked like they belonged on gingerbread houses. Thickly frosted cars sat on pristine driveways. Even the spindly tree branches were transformed, each proudly supporting a linear layer of the cold crystals. All day the downy flakes fell, and the alabaster streets remained unsullied for several hours, until someone drove out of our cul-de-sac, leaving textured tracks on the camouflaged surface. I walked in this rare, magical environment, wondering at the beauty and photographing the various comical snowmen sprouting from yards. I relished each moment, knowing that sadly the beautiful snow would vanish by morning.

An Alabama snowfall is a lovely sight to see.
Our mild, southern winters make it quite a rarity.
We're lucky if we see this beauty maybe once a year.
That's why we're so enamored for the short time that it's here.

The bread and milk have long been gone at all the grocery stores,
To prepare for days of freedom from our teachers and employers.
We track the outside temperature, willing it to fall
Enough for nature's Snow Queen to kindly on us call.

Sometimes we wake to find that snow has covered trees and ground.
Sometimes we get to watch the lacy snowflakes falling down.
But either way the children play with squeals of pure delight,
So glad their prayers were answered, and the world is frosted white.

Snowplows are nonexistent so the roads aren't very clear,
And warm and cozy houses folks are happy to stay near.
Unless with chains on tires they are brave enough to try
Driving on the white fluff that has fallen from the sky.

After walking in the wonderland, it's time to brew some tea.
On the stove my little teapot blows its whistle merrily
Beside the pot of chili I've prepared to keep us fed—
A perfect, warming snow-day meal, paired with some crusty bread.

Cuddled with a blanket, I watch my feathered friends
Flocking to the feeder to eat the tasty blend.
Their colors even brighter, against the brilliant snow,
Till one by one they to their secret nighttime shelters go.

We hope the snow will linger, and the world remain all white,
When we finally get in snuggly beds and settle for the night.
Will morning bring the sad return of trees and lawns of brown,
Or will the magic spell stay on my Alabama town?

Heaven Enough for Me

Several years ago, I was talking with a precious, elderly lady at my workplace who had lost her husband of sixty-one years. Although he had been gone for more than a decade, time had not dimmed her affection and admiration for her spouse. Her eyes sparkled as she shared her memories with me. She and her husband had been high school sweethearts, and she had never loved another man. She spoke of how kind he had been, how he had directed a children's choir at church, and how much happiness they had shared. As the conversation ended, this gentle woman mentioned heaven and how she would see her beloved there some day. Then she asked me what kind of homes we would have in that celestial city. I replied, "Oh, we will live in mansions!" Her response still echoes in my mind and is the inspiration behind this poem. She stated that she didn't need a mansion, just seeing her husband was all she wanted. Her perspective is the essence of heaven's joy: being with Jesus and our loved ones should be heaven enough for us all.

Even without heaven's mansions
Or the brilliant streets of gold,
Without a crown upon my head
Or a shiny harp to hold,

Without the fruit of eternal life
To pick from that glorious tree,
The joy I'll find in that wonderful place
Will be heaven enough for me.

Without the lion at peace with the lamb
Or that great city glittering bright,
With gigantic gates made of shimmering pearl
Or the day never turning to night,

Without all the answers to questions asked,
When those great books are open to see,
Heaven will hold such eternal peace
And be more than enough for me.

Just walking with Jesus, hand in hand,
Upon the clear crystal sea
And greeting loved ones lost before
Will be heaven enough for me.

Take Time to Take It All In

MANY YEARS AGO, A psychiatrist told me something I have never forgotten. She advised me not to overlook the small pleasures waiting to be found each day. My doctor was convinced that an awareness of joy and beauty is as vital to mental wellness as appropriate medications and psychotherapy. Her exact words were, "Find the joy." Although I am a naturally observant person, it still requires intentional focus for me to seek out the small sources of happiness around me. This task is more difficult during some seasons of life than others. But it is on days when I am struggling that I most actively cling to anything lovely or pleasurable in my environment. In fact, there are times when I latch onto seemingly insignificant but beautiful sights, sounds, smells, and feelings like a drowning man clings to a lifesaver. Even on my most trying days I endeavor to appreciate the many moments of happiness God places in my path.

When the noise of your life is so loud in your head
You can't hear yourself over the din,
There's a wealth of small blessings to clear it away.
Take time to take them all in.

The demands of the day might be looming large
And threaten to numb you within,
But don't lose your sense of wonder and awe.
Take time to take it all in.

Take in the sky full of billowing clouds
Or a single bright flower in bloom.
Take in the rhythm of rain on the roof
Or the mute and mysterious moon.

There's joy to be found in a stranger's shy smile
Or the warmth of the sun on your skin.
It will pass you right by if you don't slow your pace
And take time to take it all in.

The coolness of pillow as sleep gently comes,
The stillness as night shadows fall,
A lyric that moves you down deep in your soul,
That memory you love to recall.

These sweet, fleeting moments are waiting each day
To fill our hearts up to the brim,
And then overflowing, if only we'll just
Take time to take them all in.

Moonlight on the Water

On a beautiful November evening, my husband and I were driving from Noccalula Falls in Gadsden, Alabama, back home to Huntsville. After a lovely day of hiking and sightseeing, we were enjoying heated car seats and pleasant conversation. As we crossed the long bridge over Guntersville Lake, I noticed a shimmering light coming from my passenger side window. It was moonlight streaming down onto the water from an enormous, full moon that had just risen above the hills. I had not seen moonlight on water in years, and this beautiful sight absolutely mesmerized me. Almost immediately the following poem began to form in my mind, so there in the dark car I texted rhyming phrases to myself on my phone. All the northward way home I tracked that magnificent orb. For a moment it would disappear behind trees or be hazed over by a few filmy clouds but then to my delight pop back into view. By the time we arrived home, the robust round had ascended higher and was steadily shining its radiant light on my driveway and house. Reluctantly I went inside, wishing I could watch that luminous moon glide through the inky sky all night.

The moon has cleared the eastern hills.
I see its splendid form
Across a lake that's smooth as glass
On a night that's still and warm.

The water serves as a mirror
Reflecting faithfully,

The beams of moonglow streaming down—
Pure luminosity.

The moonlight traces a shimmering road.
A silken ribbon stretches
From one side of the shadowy lake
Till the far shore it firmly catches.

Its glare lights up the scattered clouds
Hanging so high in space.
Sometimes their thin wisps drift across
The bright moon's ancient face.

From the dark, luxurious heavens
The light pours forth from the moon
In a silent, steady torrent
That chases away the gloom.

I can't look away from this magical sight,
The moon and its glorious glow,
The way it looks touching the water
When it's giant and full and low.

Evergreen Love

THE YEARS I HAVE been employed in senior living communities have been extremely fulfilling. It is a pleasure and honor to ease the burdens and brighten the days of the residents. Still, these dear people have given so much more to me than I could ever give to them. I have often tried to describe the wave of love I sense washing over me as I walk through the door in the morning or the feeling of working in a building filled with doting grandparents. Most older people have gained incredible wisdom and insight during their many decades on this earth, and I am fortunate to be their eager student. Under their tutelage I have learned the importance of perspective, resilience, honor, and sacrifice. I have laughed at their stories, been humbled by their attitudes, marveled at their experiences, and felt inspired by their lives. I am particularly awed by the couples living in these communities who were married long before I was even born. Their devotion and dedication to each other are things I aspire to emulate in my own marriage.

The party was in full swing
As the band played catchy tunes,
At a community where seniors lived,
The room festive with balloons.

The dance floor wasn't crowded,
Just a few folks stepped and swayed.
Some required walkers but
Still danced the night away.

I stood behind a table
Where I watched and served the food,
looking 'round at smiling faces
Which reflected happy moods.

Then from the side, along the wall,
A couple slowly rose
And made their way to where the others
Held hands and tapped their toes.

The man was small and very frail
And the woman walked behind,
Her back so bent her head hung down,
But her husband helped her find

The dance floor, where he slowly turned,
His eyes all stars and sparks.
He grasped her walker and led her around
In gentle, graceful arcs.

She mostly walked, with twists and taps
As much as she could afford,
Looking up from time to time to the face
Of the man she so clearly adored.

Her smile was one that could transcend
The bonds of time and space,
Reflected in the tears now streaming
Down her husband's face.

This simply had to be
the sweetest thing I'd ever seen,
A love that after sixty years
Was fresh and evergreen.

Undaunted by the challenges
They'd met through fate or chance,
Their love propelled them to the floor
To carry on their dance.

When the Clouds Start Glowing at Sundown

MANY ADJECTIVES CAN CORRECTLY describe God, but I believe the word that best defines him is loving. God's pure love motivates everything he does. Past, present, and future, the Father's care and devotion for each of us is powerful and life changing. Every day our Maker showers us with affection and grace in countless ways. Like any caring parent, he delights in giving us gifts, both large and small. The King of Heaven grants us salvation, peace, and his presence. He brings joy into our lives through people, pets, and nature. The Author of Beauty enriches our existence with colors, aromas, and music. Right up to the moment our eyes close in sleep, God pursues us with his matchless love.

When the clouds start glowing at sundown,
Turning pink and gray and gold
On the edges of billowing whiteness,
It's a sight that never grows old.

When the clouds start glowing at sundown
Bright shafts of light stream down,
Stretching from cloud to cloud below
Like the ladder that Jacob found.

When the clouds start glowing at sundown,
And quiet descends all around
Save the sounds of the treefrogs and crickets,
The darkness drifts down to the ground.

When the clouds start glowing at sundown
Then all nature goes to her rest,
The squirrels to trees and the rabbits to burrows
And the birds to their babes in the nest.

When the clouds start glowing at sundown
And cast long last shadows on hills,
As I walk in the deepening dimness,
My spirit cannot help but thrill

At this beauty bestowed on all humans,
For God has one more word to say
About how he cares for his children
As he brings to an end one more day.

Four-Leaf Clover Prayer

Whoever composed the phrase, "The Lord works in mysterious ways" must have been a wise individual indeed. I have experienced this truth countless times in my life and also observed it in the lives of the people I know and love. This simple poem relates one of those miraculous times.

When I was young, I was strangely adept at finding clovers with four leaves, but as I grew older, possibly due to dimming eyesight and waning patience, I sadly seemed to lose this unique ability. At the time of this poem's writing, it had been many years since I triumphantly plucked one of these beaming treasures from among its common comrades.

Although the Spring weather tried its best to cheer me, I arrived home from work feeling down. Even admiring my profusion of gorgeous yellow and orange daffodils failed to brighten my mood. Suddenly, I noticed all the pesky clover crowding out the fescue in a small section of grass near my mailbox. On a whim, I decided to search for a four-leaf clover. Initially having no success, I doubtfully asked God for help, feeling guilty for making such a trivial request. These verses tell the happy ending to what I believe was a divinely orchestrated experience.

It was just a silly little thing
I asked the Lord to do
On a day I felt defeated
And my mood was sad and blue.

I know the Lord is busy
With so much on his mind.
I told him if he answered "No"
That it would be just fine.

I was kneeling near my mailbox
On a balmy day in spring,
Searching a patch of clover
For those rare four leaves of green.

Without success, methodically,
I counted each sprig's leaves,
When out of nowhere through my mind
A thought began to weave.

Would it be right to ask the God
Who lives in heaven above
For just a small assurance
Of his interest and his love

For me as I was walking
Through a dark and lonely time?
And quickly I decided
To ask his help to find

A four-leaf clover. And within
A moment, maybe two,
I found what I was looking for,
And in my heart there grew

A greater love for God
Than I had ever known before.
I left that patch of clover
With my hope and faith restored.

How mysteriously wonderful
That God would draw me closer
And touch my soul with comfort
With a tiny four-leaf clover.

Look Around

WHEN HE IS IN a public place like a restaurant, my husband insists on positioning himself facing the door. Our family has learned to let him choose his seat first, since he is uncomfortable and uneasy when his back is to the entrance of an establishment. The ability to see people entering and exiting helps my husband maintain situational awareness, which can be defined as constantly monitoring the people and actions around you to protect yourself and others from harm. I am happy to let Roddy fill this protective role, since I would find such a consciousness distracting and anxiety-provoking. However, I am passionate about another type of awareness: the keen perception of beautiful and fascinating things all around me. In fact, it is hard to imagine living without a sensitivity to all there is in my environment to enjoy. Through this poem, I urge readers to develop the habit of using one's senses to recognize, appreciate, and benefit from the countless positive sensations you will encounter every day. Pay attention. Stay alert. Keep your antennae up. And your world, too, can inspire joy.

Look around, look around, I implore, look around,
Every day of your life, look around,
Or you'll fail to see details and minutia galore
That patiently wait to be found.

The beautiful flowers for sale at the store
Can make you feel much more alive,
And don't let the blossoms on shrubbery and trees
Dissolve in a blur as you drive.

Don't be blind to the smiling baby you pass,
Held safe in the arms of his mother.
The sunset you see from the high, hilly road
Is truly unique to all others.

Listen and hear, listen and hear,
I implore you to listen and hear
Sounds you will miss if you're deaf with neglect.
They will not force their way past your ears.

Sounds like the kettle of tea on the stove,
Commencing its quaint, warning whistle.
Listen, the finch sings its song just for you,
Perched on a spiked, purple thistle.

The bright ring of laughter should never grow old.
You must bask in its warmth for a while.
Let its tinkling, tickling notes touch your lips
And shape them into a broad smile.

Breathe in the smells, breathe in the smells,
I implore you to breathe in the smells,
The aromas you may fail to benefit from
That linger or powerfully swell.

The juicy, green scent of a freshly cut lawn
That's there when you walk out your door.
A stranger's cologne, the air after rain,
The fragrance of newly mopped floors.

The tiniest whiff of a flowering shrub,
So subtle and soft and sweet.
The ground damp from sprinklers, spiced candles and soap,
The flowers that grow at your feet.

God gave us our senses so we could enjoy
Life more deeply, and wise we will be
If we don't take for granted the everyday pleasure
From what we can smell, hear, and see.

It Calls to Me

I WROTE THIS POEM on my fifty-fifth birthday while lying on the chaise lounge on my back porch. The Alabama humidity was oddly absent, causing the June weather to be especially lovely. An oak shaded my oasis, and a steady breeze stirred the leaves on the trees and maintained a perfect temperature. Although I live in town, I was enjoying a view of nearby Green Mountain and watching wildlife in the wooded area behind my house. One week prior, I had sorrowfully resigned from my position at a job I adored, due to a decline in my mental health that had begun on the first day of the year. In the few days since my resignation, I had accepted my need to be unemployed, and the bitter sadness was replaced with a profound feeling of relief. I recognized that quitting my job was an essential and necessary step in regaining wellness of mind. A few months later the darkness of depression and the paralysis of anxiety finally began to subside. I am grateful to my doctor, therapist, and family for the roles each played in my recovery. I am also thankful to the Creator for the world of nature that was so instrumental to my process of healing. Time spent outside, whether walking around my neighborhood or in the hills near my home, sitting by the pond or on my porch, gazing at the moon, or tending my flower gardens were all a large part of the self-care I needed so desperately. I was especially affected by nature during this period, and after writing infrequently over the previous months produced a flurry of poems in a matter of weeks.

It calls to me, the greenness,
The mount I see beyond,

The grass in all its lushness,
The lilting Cardinal's song.

These hushed summons of nature
Soothe my very soul.
I feel the shackles of all cares
Release their crippling hold.

The trees do not stand silent.
They laugh along with me
As I watch the squirrels and rabbits
Jump and scamper tirelessly.

Then bursts of silence leave me deaf
To every other voice.
Helpless in its power,
To resist is not a choice.

It brings a sigh to leave this place
And return to life indoors.
And just before reluctant steps begin
The voice implores,

"Please stay another moment
And listen to the wind.
It was set in motion just for you,
The trees began to bend

Because they know you need to heal
A little more today.
You need to feel the breeze's touch
And see the branches sway,

And then you'll finally be prepared
To face your life again,
Knowing soon you can return
As to a faithful friend."

Don't Forget to Look for the Moon

WHAT IS IT ABOUT the moon that makes me look for this distant, dusty rock anytime I'm outside at night? Why are my eyes inexplicably drawn to the heavens in hopes of seeing this orbiting circle of light? Maybe that ethereal and mysterious radiance? Or the varying phases, shapes, and sizes? Could it be the moon's ability to peek through clouds or be encircled by a rosy ring? I do not have answers to my ponderings. I wrote this poem at the end of December, when short days provide a larger window of opportunity to view earth's lone natural satellite in the dark sky. While walking to my car at the end of the workday, driving home, and stepping out of my car into the driveway, I search the winter sky for a glimpse of the shining celestial body. Somehow its luminous beauty never fails to surprise and delight me.

Don't forget to look for the moon,
When you're driving home late in your car.
It may be just rising, you just never know,
As you go to a place near or far.

The moon might be shining its light on your house
As you walk from your car to your door.
It takes but a moment to look to the skies.
It might not have been there before.

The moon might be balancing, silent and large,
On horizon's edge much like a ball,

Or it might be much smaller as high in the heavens
It causes dim shadows to fall.

Waxing or waning, crescent or full,
First or last quarter, or new,
And if you by chance are lucky that day,
You might catch the moon that's called blue.

Each time that I see it, its elegant glow
Both startles and calms me as I
Count my good fortune of seeing again
The beautiful moon in the sky.

Our Heavenly Father Feeds Them

IN HIS INFINITE WISDOM and compassion, our Heavenly Father recognizes that fallen human beings struggle to be assured of his love and care. He understands the faith required to believe in a being we cannot physically see, hear, or touch. So, God provides many resources to aid us in our endeavor to know him, believe his promises, and love him as a father and as a friend. The Lord gives us his inspired Word to instruct us, sends caring people to encourage us, grants the Holy Spirit to speak to us, and supplies the faith we need to connect with him and live a joyful life. Another avenue God uses to reveal himself and his purpose is the magnificent world of nature. The brilliant sunrises and sunsets, vast oceans, pattering rain, majestic trees, exquisite butterflies, and fascinating wildlife all give us glimpses of the Creator's character. Anywhere we are, from pole to pole, we cannot escape creation, which constantly proclaims his everlasting, unfailing love for his children.

Our Heavenly Father feeds them,
The little birds muted or bright.
He hears their glad songs in the morning
And guards them throughout the dark night.

He shows them the best place for nesting,
For sheltering eggs safe and warm.
He excitedly waits for their hatching
And protects the young all through the storm.

Water he gives when they're thirsty,
And sunshine to warm their cold wings,
The treetops for resting and hiding,
And songs sweet and joyful to sing.

He knows just when any should perish.
In sadness he must turn away.
It hurts him that one he created
Won't see the fresh start of the day.

We wonder at times if our Father,
The one who can't show us his face,
Sees us and shares in the sorrows
That plague our sad, pitiful race.

But we only must look out our windows
At the birds we can see everywhere.
If they are so loved and protected,
We're surely kept close in his care.

I'll Be Here

On a beautiful, mild, New Year's Eve, I lingered in the parking lot of my workplace talking with my co-worker. Our department had hosted a holiday event, and now we were heading home to celebrate with our families. Over the past few weeks I had noticed that my friend was quiet and withdrawn, and I sensed something was weighing on her. There in the deepening dusk I finally asked, "Are you alright?" She proceeded to describe the significant challenges and numbing tragedy she was currently experiencing. I listened but could offer no help or solutions, only my broken heart. You have probably felt the same way, standing with a friend, listening but helpless. The following day I wrote this poem.

For some reason, I was hesitant to gift these verses to this courageous young woman. I wanted to share my deep, sincere feelings of love and concern for her, which I had been unable to express that evening in the parking lot, but due to my quiet and insecure nature and her very private personality, I held back. Several months later I finally gave her a copy of this poignant poem. Although I never received any feedback, I'm so glad I shared these heartfelt words. I learned something from this experience that I hope I can put into practice with the next burdened individual I encounter. Be liberal with words of concern and compassion. Pour out your heart to people who are sad and struggling. Don't hold back. It may take courage, but as you follow the prompting of the Holy Spirit you will effortlessly echo the comforting messages he gives you.

I see the pain behind your eyes,
The sadness in your smile.
Your glow's a few shades muted
Like you've run a hundred miles.

You make a valiant effort
To appear to be alright,
But I can't help but sense
You're growing weary of the fight.

If I just had a magic wand
I'd tap you on the head,
And gone would be the bitter cause
Of everything you dread.

Or if I found Alladin's lamp,
We'd see if it were true
That genies really do exist
To grant your wish on cue.

Instead, my only way to help
And all I know to do
Is share a very small amount
Of all that weighs on you.

I don't mind hurting right along
Beside you, and I pray
That knowing this might bring
A bit of comfort to your day.

So, I'll be here, and though you're strong,
The strongest soul I've known,
The challenges you face
You do not have to face alone.

I won't shy away from tears,
And I'll stand with you in the fray.
I can't dispel the dark,
But I can try to light your way.

River of Clouds

My favorite way to write poetry is with paper and pen in hand, composing as I experience whatever I am putting to verse. I might have encountered some aspect of nature, been struck with an epiphany while reading or meditating, or been deeply touched by a song. At times I almost feel that a poem writes itself. Using my five senses, I take into my mind the inspiration behind the verses, simply putting down on paper what I see, hear, and feel, and sometimes even taste or smell. During my daily walks, while riding in the car, or even in the middle of the night, when an idea literally jars me awake, I capture ideas and phrases as notes on my phone. The following is one of several poems that began in my mind when I was walking outside. I paused my steps numerous times to text phrases to myself until I had composed nearly all the verses before returning home.

One day as I walked down my neighborhood streets,
I looked up as I always do
To search the wide skies for the beauty they hold,
Whether hazy or brilliantly blue.

And lo, and behold, a river of clouds,
Dark gray and streaked with the light,
Was flowing slowly and steadily on—
A majestic and glorious sight.

Through azure banks and past mountains jade,
No dam could e'er stop this strong current.

Small clumps of white clouds looked much like boats
Carried merrily along in the torrent.

I wanted to sail with them, joining the stream,
I didn't care where I would go.
I'd sit back and enjoy the most wonderful view
Of all I could see far below.

You just never know while in the outdoors
When nature will grant a surprise,
Like a mighty, advancing river of clouds
Winding its way through the sky.

Woodland Cathedral

IN NATURE, I TRULY find a sanctuary. Being outside or even gazing out my windows at the birds, landscape, and weather bring sensations of peace, safety, and God's presence, feelings that comprise the very definition of sanctuary. Observing all the beauty found outdoors evokes a uniquely complete peace. God's marvelous creation is a refuge from the chaos of this world, quieting and comforting me. Nature also provides a sacred place to worship the Creator, who intelligently and purposefully made its rich store of gifts for our enjoyment. Don't wait to go to church to worship God. As you experience the wonder of the natural world each day, offer him your praise and gratitude.

In the woods I found a cathedral,
Not constructed of lumber or stone.
It's never crowded with people.
In fact, I go there alone.

Its walls are the cool, gentle breezes,
Its columns the woody trunks tall.
Its floor isn't made out of marble
But colorful leaves in the fall.

The brilliant, blue sky forms the ceiling,
Or the branches of leafy, green trees.
Its choir a harmonious chorus
Of bird song and humming of bees.

This cathedral is perfect for worship,
Inspiring me to give praise
To the one who both made and sustains it
And opens its doors every day.

The Bottle of Tears

Hopefully you are aware that God loves and cares for us, but you may not know that the Bible specifically depicts Jesus collecting our tears in a bottle. Whether literal or figurative, this image speaks volumes regarding Christ's involvement in the pain and sorrow humans experience. To collect a person's tears, one must be physically very close, brushing the cheek to catch the salty drops dripping down. A collector of tears would see clearly the pain in the swollen eyes, feel the wetness on the sad face, and hear the anguished sobs. He would tenderly hold the trembling hands or even envelope the person in a gentle embrace. Comforting words would be spoken, love and concern would be expressed, promises to help and to stay would be made. Can you visualize this picture in your mind? Do you see yourself? Do you see God? Your Heavenly Friend wants you to understand that even though your eyes can't tangibly detect him, the Savior not only notices your tears but cherishes them. As you weep, your Maker is closer than the air you breathe. Reach out for him. Feel the Father's warm caress. Recognize his compassionate response. Rest in God's love and find comfort knowing how much he cares.

God catches each teardrop that falls from my eyes.
He uses a bottle, I'm told,
To keep them all safe, and he tucks them away.
To him they're more precious than gold.

He feels every hurt that I feel, and because
His love is so pure and so strong,

He can't help but stay by my side as I weep
And long for right's victory o'er wrong.

Some days the injustice I see all around,
The suffering that others endure,
Loneliness, tragedy, sorrow, and pain,
The illness that still lacks a cure

Threaten to wash me away in a tide
That crashes and billows and rolls.
But I reach for the light and can feel God's grace lift me
From water that's murky and cold.

I know God is working behind these dark scenes,
And my mustard seed faith is enough
To help me hang on to the hand of the One
Who will guide me through times that are tough.

Someday up in heaven when we're with the Lord,
He'll have eons of time to explain
His purpose in letting sin fill up the cup
Of evil and cause so much pain.

"I'm sorry for all of your heartaches, my child,"
He'll tenderly say with a sigh.
Together we'll pour out the bottle of tears
And then never again will I cry.

The Peach and Purple Sunset

Although I stay passionately in tune with the wonderful world of nature, she still manages to surprise me from time to time with extraordinary experiences. I may be lost in thought, busy with daily tasks, or dulled by fatigue, when she startles me with something so astonishing that I am stopped in my tracks. This poem describes such an instance. I just happened to be in the right place at precisely the right time to view the gloriously unique colors and patterns of this exquisite, ethereal sunset. I truly have never seen anything like this display before, and I will remember its breathtaking beauty for the rest of my life.

One evening as I drove along
Familiar streets towards home,
Expecting nothing special,
I allowed my thoughts to roam.

But as I made the westward turn
That I so often do,
A peach and purple sunset
Came suddenly into view.

Those particular and perfect hues
I had not seen before.
I'm not aware that there exists
The right descriptive words

To explain those glorious colors
That I could almost taste.
They somehow soaked into my eyes
And gently warmed my face.

The graceful swirls of pigment,
All mixed up with the clouds,
Transfixed, I stared at, breathless
At their power to astound.

My memory often fails me,
But I'd confidently bet
That this peach and purple sunset
I will not soon forget.

Thank You, Lord, for the Light

I AM, ADMITTEDLY, A morning person. When the long fingers of sunrise silently reach through my window blinds and gently wake me, I typically do not linger in bed. The phrase "we're burning daylight" pops into my mind and propels me to my feet. The first thing I do each morning is eagerly open my bedroom window blinds to look out. It always brings a little burst of joy to see sunshine. Although the title of one of the poems included in this book is, "There's Beauty in the Darkness," light is what my heart craves. Unless I'm looking at the varying and luminous moon, winking stars, strange and mysterious constellations, my colorful garden lights, a cozy campfire, bursting fireworks, or festive Christmas lights, I find little enjoyment in darkness. We keep the blinds on the back side of our house open at night, and I find the blank wall of blackness beyond the windows a little disconcerting. Only glowing objects make the lack of light bearable. Cataracts are beginning to dim the world around me, so I find relief in blazing light fixtures with numerous one hundred-watt bulbs while others find them irritating. The glare of my light therapy device simultaneously soothes and invigorates my mind. Mental and spiritual darkness are especially oppressive to me and can be overtaken only by the brilliant rays of God's presence, truth, and love. His light is what truly illuminates my days, my path, and my life.

When at sunset I'm already dreading the night
And longing for sunrise when all will be right,
I thank you, Lord, for the light.

When I get into bed, but I'm craving the glow
That nourishes the earth and makes everything grow,
I thank you, Lord, for the light.

When kind sunbeams wake me again in the morn
And tell me another grand day has been born,
I thank you, Lord, for the light.

When I can't see ahead, and I'm groping and blind,
As a deep midnight stalks me and invades my mind,
I thank you, Lord, for your light.

When even the darkness is not dark to you,
And you take my right hand and lead me on through,
I thank you, Lord, for your light.

When at home up in heaven we don't need the sun
But only God's glory, for forever's begun,
We'll thank you, Lord, for your light.

So, He Gave Me You

My husband and I began dating during our junior year of high school, nearly forty years ago at the time of this writing. We married halfway through college, before we transferred from a small, Christian institution to the University of Alabama. I was nineteen years old, he was twenty. I would not advise people to marry as young as we did, but in our case, we had something so special that it worked. During our years together we have exchanged very few harsh words and had even rarer fights. Hand in hand we have navigated changing careers, learned to manage money, experienced parenthood, endured heartache, and weathered numerous storms of difficulty. But what stands out most clearly is the fun we've had, the trips we have taken, and the love and laughter we have shared. Oh, how we have been blessed! I am convinced that all those years ago God miraculously plunked Roddy down into my life, where he quickly captured my heart and became my one true love. Our relationship is so rare and wonderful, it must be a gift from heaven.

God wanted to surprise me
Like loving fathers do,
With a special, unexpected gift,
And so he gave me you.

A person with a heart of gold,
Devoted, kind, and true,
Who'd make me laugh most every day,
And so he gave me you.

I didn't need a fancy car
Or a house brand spanking new,
But a rare, irreplaceable treasure,
And so he gave me you.

God could've bestowed a wealth of gold,
Millions, not a few,
But money can't bring happiness,
So instead, he gave me you.

A hand to hold, a warm embrace,
A love to help me through
Trials that would surely come,
And so he gave me you.

You've made my life joyful and full
Like only you could do.
I feel the deepest gratitude
Because he gave me you.

I Can't Let You Go

My son's wedding day was approaching rapidly. Before I knew it, only weeks remained until the happy occasion. But as the momentous day drew nearer, I was overwhelmed by a feeling of tremendous loss. I couldn't stop thinking about my son's childhood days, how we could never go back, and how things would never be the same. My grief left my emotions raw and ragged. Visiting with my son or even thinking about the wedding induced tears. It seemed an extreme and even ridiculous response to such a positive and common event. I told myself that I wanted my son to be independent and find happiness with someone. I scolded myself for being ungrateful. I compared myself to parents who lose a child to addiction, disease, or even suicide. I journaled, prayed, talked about it with my husband, and even saw my therapist. But nothing helped. I began to dread the wedding, worried I would break down and embarrass myself, or worse, detract from the ceremony. It was during this difficult time that I wrote these verses, which reflect no resolution, only the painful impasse where I found myself. It was as if my son was a little boy again, trying to pry off my fingers from around his small, sweaty hand so he could walk alone. Except now it was my heart that held on so tightly.

It seems not long ago,
And I never was the same.
I held you gently in my arms
And softly said your name.

And just like that you took your place
So deep inside my heart.
I never even thought about
The day we'd be apart.

Throughout the years my world revolved
Around you night and day.
Your wondrous face, your brilliant mind—
They took my breath away.

I watched you change into a man.
I watched you learn and grow.
And now it's time to spread your wings,
Yet I can't let you go.

Go to take ahold of all
Your heart is dreaming of.
You've found your independence.
You've found someone to love.

Although it's all a part of what
I've always wished for you,
The time has come too quickly,
And I can't seem to do

The thing that must be done today.
It's for the best, I know.
You're not a child anymore,
But I can't let you go.

Rainy July Day

Summers are notoriously hot and humid in Alabama, with temperatures approaching one hundred degrees, and the heat index easily exceeding that number. Droughts are also common in the summer months, with no rain falling for weeks at a time. We had endured an extremely dry period when this poem was written. After a lovely June, July had arrived, bringing stifling heat and minimal precipitation. Only faithful watering kept my flowers alive, and the birdbath was especially busy. Even with regular waterings from the sprinkler system, our yard browned and frowned, and the trees drooped hopelessly in the shimmering air. By the end of the month, we were all wondering how we would survive August. Then, miraculously, came the rain. The delicious drops fell intermittently all day, cooling and moistening everything they touched. I kept busy in my house until this poem came to mind. Sitting down at my dining room table, I watched the glorious downpour and wrote these verses.

A peaceful, rainy, July day
We had not long ago,
When scorching sun gave sweet reprieve
To everything below.

Animals, plants, and humans, too,
Were stilled by thunder rumbling.
Birds sang in whispers in the trees.
The bees all paused their bumbling.

The juicy drops fell randomly,
Their "tap, tap" very low.
The sky was somber, a welcome change
From its cheerful, blinding glow.

The grateful, parched, and waiting land
Released a smell profound
In thanks to moisture soaking through
The thirsty, grassy ground.

A few brave robins couldn't resist
To gather the worms a-climbing
Up to the surface of the earth
To escape the liquid rising.

A lovely time was had by all,
Although the sky was gray.
Refreshing and reviving
Was that rainy July day.

Have You Ever Had a Friend

As an introvert, I have a small but precious circle of friends. It's hard to imagine life without these dear individuals. My best friend who lived only a few miles from me recently moved out of state, but we maintain our close relationship through calls, texts, cards, and visits. Some of my comrades are former co-workers who I still interact with regularly. There is also a select group of residents living in the senior living community where I worked with whom I formed tender bonds. I depend on all these wonderful souls for unconditional love, judgement-free society, advice, laughter, and joy. They provide the connection with others that I crave. But the ally I depend on the most is my Heavenly Friend, Jesus. The ultimate of companions, what a comfort and blessing he is in all seasons of my life, incapable of ever letting me down or failing to enrich each day. Though unseen, he is always there, holding my hand and my heart as I traverse the road of life.

Have you ever had a friend
Who loves you through and through
And always lends a hand
In whatever it is you do?

Have you ever had a friend
Who's right there by your side
In good times and in bad,
A true and faithful guide?

Have you ever had a friend,
A person who will share
All your hopes and every dream
And show you that he cares?

Have you ever had a friend
Who calms your dread and fears
And reassures you always
He'll be there throughout the years?

Have you ever had a friend?
If so, then you are blessed
With a life enriched in many ways
And doubled happiness.

Blow, Wind, Blow

On a warm, windy day when I was feeling blue, I sat on my front porch and wrote this simple poem. The composition was my heart's cry of frustration, born of the maddening, mysterious low moods that my mental health condition can cause with no basis, affiliated situation, or logical explanation. The cathartic words tumbled one after the other out of my mind and onto the paper, and composing them into rhymes calmed and comforted me. If you look beneath the surface of these verses, you will see that I am not beseeching the wind but the one whom the wind obeys. The Creator of the wind. My Creator. He who knows my every thought and all the desires of my heart. God heard my prayer that day, and I felt him come very near to me with the love, grace, and goodness that are uniquely his.

Blow, wind, blow.
Blow my blues away.
I don't know why a melancholy
Mood plagues me today.

Blow away the cobwebs
That clutter up my mind,
The questions, fears, and longings
That I always seem to find.

I don't need any answers,
Just the peace your roar can bring.

I simply need the soothing song
That only you can sing.

Keep me in this moment,
Listening only to your sound,
Until I stop my wandering thoughts,
And I can feel the ground

Of the firm and perfect present
Underneath my weary feet.
Until I can see the beauty
That makes this life complete.

Oh, blow, wind, blow.
Blow my blues away.
I don't know why a melancholy
Mood plagues me today.

Nature's Voice

I BELIEVE ALL HUMANS were created for an important reason: to provide friendship and adoration for God. Our lives will only be meaningful when we have a relationship with our Creator, and spending time with him will automatically inspire our love and worship. Nature sets a wonderful example for us to follow. From the tiniest insect to the stars in the heavens, everything in the great outdoors glorifies our Heavenly Father and inspires us to do the same. Just as God's created works proclaim his care, ingenuity, and power, we can also manifest the Lord's character to those around us with our words and actions. Our glorious Creator is more than worthy of the testimony of praise that we are called to give him.

Nature has a sacred voice
But doesn't speak with words.
Every day, by all mankind
Her exultations can be heard.

Like a grand and swelling orchestra
Or the lyrics of a song,
She worships him who made the earth.
The strains go on and on.

She tells of the Creator,
As the glowing sun shines bright,
And persists in what she has to say
As stars come out at night.

The mountains, fields, and flowers
To God their voices raise,
Making up the varied verses
Of her poetry of praise.

All the Lord's creation
Exist to adore their King,
From the vast and rolling oceans
To the tiny birds that sing.

So, if the world of nature
Gives God glory every day,
Shouldn't his crowning workmanship
Have even more to say?

Goodbye, Old Oak

Even to ardent nature lovers, my forming a bond with a tree and mourning its loss may appear extreme. In my defense, I live in town, and although it is a lovely, hilly area with ample foliage, I am also surrounded by houses and roads. I do not live out in the country, on a remote mountain, or in a lush forest. Maybe my suburban environment makes me especially appreciative of the natural beauty that exists around me. Every shapely tree, fragrant shrub, distant mountain, clump of flowers, and pristine lawn is precious to me, bringing daily pleasure. One massive oak in a postage stamp-sized yard has significant impact, and its disappointing demise would logically leave a bleak, lonely space. Certain species of timber routinely outlive humans, but some of these bark-covered giants simply do not survive long enough to suit me.

Goodbye, Old Oak,
A fine friend you have been,
Faithfully standing your post.
Your calming presence continually there
When my aching heart needed you most.

Just seeing your stately, towering frame
From my second-floor windows so high,
And gazing at branches endlessly reaching
And seeming to touch the blue sky

Caused me to pause what I thought must be done
And admire you as long as I dared.

I imagined your loving smile shining on me.
I rejoiced in the bond that we shared.

The decades have watched you flourish and thrive,
Mighty and strong and free.
Sadly, none on this earth are immortal,
Including a massive, grand tree.

But as your life ends, your giving won't cease.
As your body melts into the earth
You will lavish yourself on the hungering soil
And assist in another tree's birth.

I'll never forget all you were through the years.
Your friendship will be sorely missed.
How lucky I was to be blessed all this time
By your many and magical gifts.

The Girl I Once Was

I AM A VERY private person and rarely share my darkest thoughts and feelings with even my closest family members. Doing so leaves me feeling exposed, burdensome, and ashamed. Although this piece poured effortlessly from my pen, it is the hardest one to offer up, these verses that I hesitated to publish. You, dear reader, may wonder why I did. I have taken an uncharacteristic, calculated risk, hoping that someone who is struggling will read these words and find comfort in knowing that you are not alone. I have also endured pain and despair privately. At the time this poem was written, I was longing to reach the end of an agonizing tunnel of depression and hoping to find my true self there. I am happy to report that through God's grace I eventually did. His grace can bring you through your own dark tunnel of difficulty as well.

The girl I was is gone.
To where, I do not know.
I didn't see her leave
Or tell her she could go.

Somewhere along my path
She quietly went away.
I never would have thought
She wasn't here to stay.

So happy and so grateful,
She greeted each day's sun.

She said a prayer and then went out
To smile at everyone.

She noticed every bird
And leaf and bud and tree.
The earth and rain and sighing breeze
To her were family.

But when my fears and my regrets
Overwhelmed my mind,
And I couldn't see the past remained
A tape without rewind,

My soul sank down in blackness
And she didn't come with me.
She slipped away as darkness fell,
And I just couldn't see

A way to climb out of the hole,
A way to find the light,
That in the past had led me
And kept my spirits bright.

As I became more jaded,
I lost my faith, and then
I lost all hope I'd ever see
The girl I was again.

Is there a way to find her,
That spirit full of love?
The girl who was determined
To always rise above

Her heartaches and her struggles
And see that good abounds

In every situation,
If we just look around?

I know she's out there waiting
Patiently, because
She clings to hope that I'll become
The girl that I once was.

Kings of the Air

The story behind these verses is related by the poem itself. Central to the narrative is the contrast between the flight of a bird and the flight of an airplane. Although both feats are miraculous and even operate under the same principles of physics, they could not be more different. I believe this distinction exists because the flight of airplanes was engineered by humans, whereas the flight of birds was engineered by God. Airplanes are clearly a poor attempt at the Creator's fantastically superior design of our feathered friends. The Father's ingenuity, artistry, and unlimited ability were gloriously displayed when he created our world and everything in it, and in my opinion, flying creatures are one of his most magnificent accomplishments.

I sat in an airplane looking out
The small window next to my seat
At the bustling workers milling about,
Preparing for what's no small feat.

A lumbering, creaking, metal tin can
Lifting slowly up off the dry dirt,
Then flying so far, so high, and to where?
Nearly any place on God's green earth.

When a smaller commotion somehow caught my eye.
Just over the building there flew
Two little birds, small black forms in the sky.
Maybe no other soul knew

They were there. But I eagerly watched them
Twist, turn and soar, and then wheel.
Catching a very fine breakfast—
A fresh, unaware-insect meal.

I sensed little effort, could imagine no sound
Their small wings might possibly make.
No clanking or creaking, just the whistle of air
So quietly stirred in their wakes.

Weighing so little, with light, fragile bones
And tiny, soft, feathery wings,
Engineered by their wise, loving Maker
Specifically for this one thing:

To not only fly but to move like the wind
With acrobat antics so rare.
Aerial masters to do as they please,
Born to be kings of the air.

Beauty in the Darkness

Beauty and darkness are an unlikely pair, a combination we may not always recognize. The beauty we see in shadows can be different, uncanny, and surprising. Strangely, the lack of light makes certain things attractive. The blackness highlights and at some level defines certain objects that we appreciate and enjoy. Joy from darkness. Joy in darkness. Beyond a mere observation there is a lesson to be found. Not only can unique and valuable insights be gained in times of struggle and pain but also actual gladness. Blessings may come in the form of an answered prayer, the love and care of family and friends, a deeper understanding of God, or an expanded faith in his promises. The dimness itself is not beautiful, but there are certain gifts that only darkness can bring.

There's beauty in the darkness
All throughout the year,
In colored lights that shine so bright
When Christmastime is here.

The stars are only visible
In the velvet black of night.
The sunshine makes them disappear.
They fade in warm daylight.

The moon is just an outline
In brilliant skies of blue,
But nighttime comes, and then it glows
As only it can do.

Fireworks are not the same
Till evening shadows fall,
When they burst with noise and color
And delight us one and all.

So, in life and circumstance
The dark times often provide
Special beauty only found when
Shadows the sunshine hide.

Peggy's Poem

My mother-in-law, Peggy, passed away unexpectantly on March 5, 2024, and I wrote this poem for her memorial service. After five years of miscarriages, she and my father-in-law adopted my husband, Roddy, in 1968. Peggy loved to relate the experience of driving to Florida to pick up her long-awaited baby. In that pre-car seat era, she held him on her lap all the way back to Alabama, gazing at her very own perfect, beautiful newborn. Peggy delighted in her role as a caring and devoted mother and later gave birth to two more sons.

I met Peggy soon after Roddy and I started dating in high school, and she instantly loved and accepted me. After I became a mother, my appreciation and respect for her deepened drastically, as I began to understand the profound generosity required to share a son's love with a daughter-in-law. In addition to showing this beneficence, Peggy gave me the irreplaceable gift of loving my children with all her heart. Sam and Ben had the grandmother of every child's dreams. Oh, how Nanny doted on my boys, relishing every moment she spent with them.

Unfortunate circumstances brought great challenges in Peggy's later years, and Roddy became her dedicated caregiver until she died. Now our family eagerly awaits the coming of Jesus, when we will be reunited with this dear lady. Then our time with Peggy will continue throughout the joyful ages of eternity.

The things she always wanted
To do the most in life

Were simple, pure, and noble—
To be a mother and a wife.

Her wedding day had come and gone.
You could see it in her eyes,
Anticipation of the day
When she'd be singing lullabies.

Then came disappointments
That caused her many tears.
She refused to become bitter
Or give in to grief or fear.

The Lord had someone special
Chosen for her all the while.
Before she even met him
He was already her child.

After five long years of waiting,
She held him all the way.
Not how she first imagined
She became a mom that day.

Oh, what joy he brought her,
A baby of her own.
This child erased forever
All the sorrow she had known.

As he grew up, she loved and cared
For him as few moms can.
Their bond grew strong and never dimmed,
Once he became a man.

And though her final years brought
Both of them some trying days,

He couldn't bear to think about
The day she'd go away.

When they meet some day in heaven,
She'll hold her boy again.
He made his mom a mother,
And that love will never end.

How Beautiful Heaven Must Be

GOD DID NOT ALLOW the blight of sin to completely erase the glory of his creation. He preserved abundant beauty for us to enjoy. Our Heavenly Father must have anticipated how much we would need the loveliness found outdoors, and how the majesty of nature would inspire us to love and praise him. The Creator must have foreseen the peace that would wash over our souls when viewing a vivid sunset, the delight we would feel observing elusive wildlife, and the fascination we would experience identifying the dazzling array of birds frequenting our feeders. He ordained the hope a glorious sunrise would instill in our hearts, the awe the vast seas and soaring mountains would inspire, and the wonder delicate butterflies and exquisite flowers would evoke. God provided not just one or two types of plants but numerous varieties of trees, flowers, and mosses, along with thousands of species of animals. What then will we experience in heaven? The answer is found in the Bible, where we learn that not even in our wildest dreams can we fathom what the natural world will resemble in our eternal home.

We're told what God has prepared up above
Is nothing like we've ever seen
Or heard with our ears or even conceived
In our wildest, most fantastic dream.

But when I observe on a bright springtime morn
The sunlight caressing each tree,

I can't help but question the obvious truth
Of how beautiful heaven must be.

When I hear the sweet singing and various calls
Of the birds in melodious keys,
I wonder what birdsong will sound like up there.
How beautiful can heaven be?

When I feel the firm sand and the powerful surf
And gaze at the brilliant blue sea,
It's amazing to think of the ocean up there
And how beautiful heaven must be.

When I'm out in the garden, tending my plants
With the damp soil under my knees,
I look forward to smelling celestial blooms
And how beautiful heaven must be.

When my soul sings in wonder at all God has made,
In my heart there springs forth jubilee,
As I think of the joy in that wonderful place
And dream of what heaven must be.

New Year's Eve

THE VALUE OF TIME is often unappreciated by youth. Many young people feel invincible and see the road of life stretching securely and endlessly ahead. But as our allotted days tick swiftly by, the number of gray hairs and wrinkles increases, the children grow up and move away, and the end of life draws nearer, the precious nature of time is recognized. With age comes wisdom, wisdom that instructs us to tread thoughtfully the path that lies ahead, savoring each day and living it with purpose. Wasting precious minutes makes us feel uncomfortable, and our definitions for both squandering time and living well evolve. New Year's Eve becomes less of a celebration and more of a solemn reminder of the finite nature of life. We don't resolve to lose weight or read more or work less, but to be more grateful, gracious, and intentional. To slow our pace and get off the merry-go-round when needed. To be faithful stewards of the days that remain, so that when our last hour comes, we will feel satisfaction instead of regret.

The time has come again
When we gently turn the page,
To start another chapter
In the book of all our days.

In the quiet dark of midnight
As we watched the timepiece face,
The sand ran out on one more year,
And a new one took its place.

This milestone can't be ignored,
Although it doesn't seem
That anything has changed at all
In the time that was between.

This night more than all others,
As only New Year's can,
Reminds us that time marches on
E'er since the world began.

For time is really all we have
That no one can make more of.
That precious, rare commodity
All have a measured store of.

This year how will we spend it?
In a flippant, careless way?
Or treasuring and guarding
Every moment of each day?

The year's been set in motion,
And only time will tell
As the seconds fly by swiftly
If we will live it well.

The Brave and Hopeful Beauty of the Soul

I AM BLESSED WITH a keen sensitivity to joy and beauty, overwhelmed by achingly beautiful music, vibrant art, poignant literature, and the fantastic world of nature. This awareness can have a darker side, because I also feel my own pain and the pain of others very acutely. Even if only briefly, I am greatly affected by any sadness or hurt encountered. Overhearing a child being harshly chastised by a parent or passing a crushed animal on the road sends a sharp pang through my heart as tears well up in my eyes. Many would label me "overreactive" or "too sensitive."

When hurt by another person, I initially feel intense pain, loneliness, and even despair, but then as I cling to Jesus those feelings are replaced by comfort and hope. Wishing I could skip the first reaction, I'm a bit embarrassed that I have temporarily lost sight of God's unfathomable love and care for me. Thankfully, I know my Heavenly Friend kindly and patiently understands. I always emerge from the blackness with a sparkling clarity that comes from leaning on the Lord and realizing that I am never alone, regardless of my feelings.

When I'm feeling so abandoned and wincing from the sting
Of betrayal by a person I hold dear,
I long for blessed freedom from devotion, strong and true,
The reward of which is but a thousand tears,

Hot and wet and slow and quiet, christening the skin,
Threatening to wash my soul away.

I cling to God Almighty in my blind and raging grief,
And only hope he hears me when I pray.

The pain is very private but could possibly be eased
By a kind word I would value more than gold,
But selfish needs and motives raise a pallid hand instead
And cause my fragile house of cards to fold.

The ones I love the fullest can cause the deepest wounds,
But I must remember who is always there.
It's Jesus, who brings healing balm and holds me while I weep
And answers every desperate, silent prayer.

He'll touch each hopeless puzzle piece of pain I now despair
To ever bring again to something whole
And miraculously move them till they form what once was there:
The brave and hopeful beauty of the soul.

www.ingramcontent.com/pod-product-compliance
Lightning Source LLC
Chambersburg PA
CBHW060400050426
42449CB00009B/1823